SPORTS SUPERSTARS

WHO IS LIONEL MESSI?

PERCY LEED

Lerner Publications ◆ Minneapolis

Statistics in this book are accurate through June 1, 2025.

Lerner Publications Company
An imprint of Lerner Publishing Group, Inc.
241 First Avenue North
Minneapolis, MN 55401 USA

For reading levels and more information, look up this title at www.lernerbooks.com.

Main body text set in Mikado.
Typeface provided by HvD Fonts.

Editor: Annie Zheng **Designer:** Mary Ross **Photo Editor:** Evan Villas

Library of Congress Cataloging-in-Publication Data

Names: Leed, Percy, 1968- author
Title: Who is Lionel Messi? : soccer superstar / Percy Leed.
Description: Minneapolis : Lerner Publications, 2026. | Series: Lerner sports rookie. Sports superstars | Includes bibliographical references and index. | Audience: Ages 5–8 | Audience: Grades K–1 | Summary: "Lionel Messi is one of the best soccer players ever. He has won 10 La Liga titles, and in 2022, he led Argentina to victory at the World Cup. Learn more about his career"— Provided by publisher.
Identifiers: LCCN 2025019538 (print) | LCCN 2025019539 (ebook) | ISBN 9798765689615 library binding | ISBN 9798348029111 paperback | ISBN 9798765697863 epub
Subjects: LCSH: Messi, Lionel, 1987- —Juvenile literature | Soccer players—Argentina—Biography—Juvenile literature | LCGFT: Biographies
Classification: LCC GV942.7.M398 L44 2026 (print) | LCC GV942.7.M398 (ebook) | DDC 796.334092—dc23/eng/20250624

LC record available at https://lccn.loc.gov/2025019538
LC ebook record available at https://lccn.loc.gov/2025019539

Manufactured in the United States of America
1-1012762-54829-6/30/2025

TABLE OF CONTENTS

SUPER SCORER

It was the fourth game of the 2025 MLS season. Inter Miami was down 1–0 against Atlanta.

Lionel Messi kicked the ball above the Atlanta goalkeeper's head. It went in! Messi's goal made the score 1–1.

Lionel Messi was born on June 24, 1987.

He grew up in Rosario, Argentina.

Soccer is a big sport in Argentina. Messi quickly became the best player in Rosario.

When he was 13, he met with scouts from a soccer team in Spain. They offered him a spot on their team.

He moved from Argentina to Barcelona, Spain. He made the top Barcelona team at 16.

Messi won his first Golden Ball award in 2009. The Golden Ball goes to the best player in men's soccer.

In 2012, he set a record for most goals in a year. He scored 91 goals.

Winning a World Cup
was Messi's dream.

He almost won the World Cup in 2014. He led Argentina into the final match against Germany.

But Germany won 1–0.

Argentina lost again in the 2018 World Cup.

Then, in 2022, it finally happened. Messi led Argentina to the World Cup Final.

The team played France. Argentina won 4–2 and took home the World Cup!

Messi has switched teams a few times in his career.

He joined Inter Miami in 2023.

In 2024, he scored 20 goals in 19 games. Messi is a superstar! Fans can't wait to see him score more goals.

LIONEL MESSI
CAREER STATS

PRO GAMES: **933**

PRO GOALS: **757**

GOLDEN BALL AWARDS: **8**

PRO LEAGUE TITLES: **12**

LIONEL MESSI

GEAR

GLOSSARY

MLS: Major League Soccer

scout: a person who judges the skills of athletes

World Cup: the most important event in pro soccer

LEARN MORE

Laughlin, Kara L. *Soccer.* The Child's World, 2023.

Perry, Caroline L. *Messi's Magic: How Lionel Messi Became the Greatest Soccer Player of All Time.* Scholastic, 2025.

Wagner, Zelda. *Soccer Superstars.* Lerner Publications, 2025.

INDEX

PHOTO ACKNOWLEDGMENTS

Image credits: Andrew J. Clark/ISI Photos/Getty Images, pp. 5, 23; AlexPhotoStock/Getty Images, p. 7; Marcelo Boeri/El Grafico/Getty Images, p. 8; Denis Doyle/Getty Images, p. 11; LLUIS GENE/AFP via Getty Images, p. 12; Matthias Hangst/Getty Image, p. 14; Mike Hewitt/FIFA via Getty Images, p. 17; Marc Atkins/Getty Image, p. 18; Kevin C. Cox/Getty Images, p. 21. Design element: liangpv/Getty Images.
Cover image: AP Photo/Rebecca Blackwell.